GUIDE TO

Performance Evaluation of Serials Vendors

ASSOCIATION FOR LIBRARY COLLECTIONS & TECHNICAL SERVICES

SERIALS SECTION ACQUISITIONS COMMITTEE

AMERICAN LIBRARY ASSOCIATION

Chicago and London 1997

Composition by Dianne M. Rooney in Times and
Helvetica using QuarkXpress 3.32 for Macintosh
7100/66

Printed on 50-pound Finch Opaque, a pH-neutral
stock, and bound in 10-point Scott Index cover
stock by IPC, St. Joseph, MI

The paper used in this publication meets the minimum requirements of American National Standard
for Information Sciences—Permanence of Paper for
Printed Library Materials, ANSI Z39.48-1992. ∞

ISBN: 0-8389-3469-2

Printed in the United States of America.

01 00 99 98 97   5 4 3 2 1

Contents

Acknowledgments

At the American Library Association 1987 Annual Conference, the Resources and Technical Services Division (now the Association for Library Collections and Technical Services) Serials Section Acquisitions Committee agreed to prepare and publish guidelines for evaluating the performance of serials vendors. From 1988 to 1993, the committee has had six chairs who have led the committee through this project and others: Marjorie Adams, Myrna McCallister, Jana Lonberger, Richard Brumley, Joyce McDonough, and Marifran Bustion. As a first step, members drafted outlines for the original sections: Marjorie Adams, Richard Brumley, Lynn Cummins, October Ivins, Myrna McCallister, Frank Orser, and Wilba Swearingen. Orser and McCallister surveyed vendors regarding criteria. The first draft was prepared by Wilba Swearingen and October Ivins in June 1990; Ivins prepared subsequent drafts.

The thoughtful comments of many members on each draft have vastly improved the document. Those who commented are Richard Brumley, Susan Davis, Julia Gammon, Leslie Knapp, Jana Lonberger, and Lisa Peterson, with substantial comments provided by Marifran Bustion and Gary J. Brown. The annotated bibliography was also a group effort, edited initially by Wilba Swearingen, updated by Susan Davis, and completed by Marifran Bustion, with annotations contributed by them and Marjorie Adams, Gary J. Brown, Lynn Cummins, October Ivins, Frank Orser, and Lisa Peterson. Additional sources are acknowledged in the bibliography.

The committee is indebted to other members of the Association for Library Collections and Technical Services, publishers, and vendors who commented on the fifth draft. The comments of Vivian Buell, Ballen; Rita VanAssche Bueter, Blackwell North America; Janice Fleming, American Institute of Physics; Pam Laurell, Book House; William Leazer, Majors; Donna Lively, University of Texas at Arlington; Jane Maddox, Harrassowitz; Barbara Meyers, Meyers Consulting; Joyce Ogburn, Yale University; Leonard Schrift, Ballen; Andrew Shroyer, New York University; John Tagler, Elsevier Science; and Antoon Van Velzen, Swets, are gratefully acknowledged.

I. Introduction

This guide is designed to aid serials managers and library administrators in conducting serials vendor performance evaluations. Serials vendors, publishers, and library automated system vendors are a secondary audience for the guide. It describes the factors to be considered before beginning a review and explains criteria that may be utilized. The guide suggests methodologies for single criterion evaluations and for comprehensive reviews that study multiple aspects of vendor performance. It includes an annotated bibliography.

It appears that, in practice, most serials vendor evaluations have been undertaken when a crisis situation, such as an obvious drop in performance, forces attention to specific problems. The committee recommends that vendor evaluation be incorporated into the regular work flow and that clear objectives for vendor performance be established and communicated to vendors. We are confident that the availability of this guide will encourage better evaluation of serials vendors.

Because the application of serials automation varies widely among automated systems and because not all libraries have fully automated serials acquisitions, these guidelines address which aspects should be studied and the types of data that should be collected. The guidelines do not identify specific methods of data collection.

Automated serials systems can greatly aid a library conducting a serials vendor evaluation. A system can track many quantitative factors and facilitate collection and organization of data for further analysis. While computerized systems can generate reports, the quality of reports can be only as accurate as the data entered. An automated system can tabulate, for example, total claiming activity and produce reports that tabulate claims by publisher, frequencies of publication, numbers of repeated claims, and related data.

Collecting similar information in a manual system is extremely labor intensive; manual studies are more likely to be restricted to sampling than to analyses based on the measurement of total activity in any category. Libraries without automated support may conduct their studies differently than those with automated systems, but the planning and analysis guidelines are similar.

Background

Although the need to perform serials vendor evaluation has been enthusiastically acknowledged by committee members and others who have followed our work, the committee found this project a difficult undertaking. In 1987, we began planning the guide with the knowledge that there were only four published studies of serials vendor performance evaluation. We planned to identify additional unpublished studies, to encourage publication of studies, and to conduct studies ourselves as a practical basis for designing methodologies. Our spectacular lack of success in identifying additional studies made us realize that a guide was needed not just to standardize or improve studies, but to generate them.

As of late 1994, there were no additional published studies, and only four unpublished studies were identified. We conducted limited studies and these provided some guidance. As a result, this guide has a different focus and is more philosophical in tone than its counterpart, the *Guide to Performance Evaluation of Library Materials Vendors* (Chicago: ALA, 1988).

Our work is influenced by that of the Resources and Technical Services Division/Association for Library Collections and Technical Services Resources Section Collection Management and Development and Acquisitions Committees, who developed the *Guide to Performance Evaluation of Library Materials Vendors*. The title is somewhat misleading; the scope of the guide as described in its foreword is "evaluating the performance of vendors of in-print monographs." The committee has used this guide as a starting point and refers to it for information regarding the analysis of quantitative measures.

Definitions and Usage in This Document

Definitions for many of the practical and colloquial terms used in communication among librarians, vendors, and publishers who participate in the serials acquisition chain are not available in the *ALA Glossary of Library and Information Science* (Chicago: ALA, 1983) and other published sources. The committee developed a lengthy glossary of these terms which is published separately. A few key terms used in this document are defined here.

Serial: A publication in any medium issued in successive parts bearing numerical or chronological designations and intended to be continued indefinitely. Serials include periodicals; newspapers; annuals (reports, yearbooks, etc.); the journals, memoirs, proceedings, transactions, etc., of societies; and numbered monographic series. (This formal definition does not include loose-leaf services, unnumbered monographic series, and sets, but these types of publications may also be obtained on subscription or standing order, which means each volume is billed as issued.)

In this document, reference is made to *periodical subscriptions and standing orders for nonperiodical serials.* Please refer to "Serials Types and Acquisitions," p. 8, for additional discussion of these terms.

Vendor: The general, all-inclusive term used to refer to the individuals or companies, other than publishers, from whom library materials are purchased. A distinction is normally made between book vendors (also called booksellers, dealers, or jobbers) and serials vendors (also called agents or subscription agents). *Serials vendors* offer convenient purchasing and consolidated invoicing of periodical and serial titles from diverse publishers. *Book vendors* provide one convenient source for buying the books of numerous publishers; they may handle approval plans. Both types of vendors ordinarily provide the added services of claiming, order status reports, and a variety of customer services such as management reports; additional services are often available. Periodical publishers ordinarily require payment with the order. Because serials vendors usually pay publishers in advance when placing periodical orders, libraries are invoiced before receipt of material. Book vendors are expected to prepay less frequently, usually by noncommercial publishers; they normally invoice the library as material is shipped. Many serials and book vendors can also supply nonperiodical serials, such as numbered and unnumbered monographic series, irregular serials, sets, and conference proceedings.

Note the following terms used in this document:

1. *Vendor,* or *serials vendor,* used without additional description, refers to both *subscription agents* and *standing order vendors.*
2. The term *subscription agent* is used in discussions of the supply of periodical subscriptions. Subscription agents typically assess *service charges.*
3. The term *standing order vendor* is used in discussions of the supply of nonperiodical serials *by either subscription agents or book dealers.* Although there are exceptions, ordinarily subscription agents assess *service charges* for standing orders, while book dealers may offer *discount rates* for standing orders.

II. Reasons to Perform a Serials Vendor Evaluation

Two primary goals underlie the many reasons to conduct a serials vendor performance evaluation. The first is to judge the vendor's adherence to the terms of and conditions set forth for doing business. The second goal is to assess the library's accountability in providing effective service to its clientele and responsible stewardship of funds. These two fundamental goals support the five more-specific reasons discussed in this section. Education is a valuable by-product or benefit. All parties—library staff, vendors, and publishers—will benefit from learning more about their own and each other's practices.

1. *Improve Vendor Performance and Identify Cost-Effective Services.* With appropriate methodology, studies can compare the performance of multiple vendors, track one vendor's performance over time, or evaluate the service a single vendor provides for different types of orders. Once problems are documented with clear, fair, and quantitative facts, the serials manager can make specific requests for improvement. The performance analysis provides the vendor with useful feedback on weaknesses of its staff, procedures, or policies. The knowledge that evaluations are undertaken objectively and routinely should motivate vendors to improve services and promote changes and improvements throughout the industry. Positive evaluations can encourage continued good performance and can affect libraries' expectations of improved service. Effective feedback helps vendors determine which services are the most viable and cost-effective and thus assists them in controlling their costs and corresponding service charges or discount rates.

2. *Identify the Most Cost-Effective Combination of Service Provided and Service Charge/Discount Rate Assessed; Provide Data in Bid Situations.* Performance evaluations can demonstrate whether the service received from a vendor is appropriate for the service charge or discount rate in effect. With better information about services received, libraries can negotiate for more appropriate service charges or discount rates from present vendors and can anticipate and avoid changes in practice that might result in an increased cost. The service/cost combination can also be considered in selecting additional or alternative vendors and in analyzing bids. For example, if a subscription agent with a low service charge also has a high incidence of service failures that affect supply, the resulting costs in staff time and of replacement issues must also be taken into account in determining the full cost of that vendor's service. Similarly, a standing order vendor may offer an attractive discount rate but have a relatively high rate of nonsupply of new volumes, requiring close library monitoring.

The value of vendor-provided services can be compared to similar services provided through automated library systems. A vendor's automated system is designed to communicate with thousands of publishers and libraries, thereby tracking claim requests and recording supply and response information for many more transactions than those of a particular library. An automated system designed for use in a library should be able to provide management reports (of prices, claiming activity, etc.) for all library subscriptions and standing orders, not just one vendor's list. Such reports might be more readily customized and more frequently created than is presently the case with vendor-supplied management reports.

3. *Improve Supply Rates and Timeliness of Serials Receipts.* Although improvement in supply rates and the timeliness of receipts is expected, a vendor performance evaluation cannot solve all receipt problems for all serials titles. Ongoing or occasional problems can result from circumstances beyond any party's control, such as political turmoil, strikes, or natural disasters in the country of publication or the locale of the library. Procedural problems or staffing changes in the delivery system (government and commercial mail services, institutional mail distribution and delivery, and the library mailroom) can also cause delays or even nonreceipt. Persistent service difficulties with specific titles or publishers should prompt an investigation into the exact cause of the problem. Once the cause is determined, alternative strategies may be warranted, such as changing the vendor, working directly with the publisher, publicizing the publisher's practice, seeking mediation from the ALCTS Publisher/Vendor/Library Relations Committee, or referring the problem title to collection development staff for possible cancellation or substitution.

4. *Improve Library Procedures and Provide Better Management Information.* A well-planned study can reveal library work flow or procedural problems that need to be corrected. Increased accountability of all library practices requires assessing library performance in terms of services provided rather than by traditional output measurements and usage statistics. Restricted library budgets create an urgent need to expend library funds effectively. For example, an annual directory that arrives from a publisher or vendor four months after publication has lost one-third of its usefulness and is not an effective use of library funds. As staffing levels in library technical services operations continue to decline, making effective use of staff time, avoiding duplication of effort, streamlining work flow, and minimizing time required to deal with problems and errors become increasingly important. Evaluations can provide useful information for automation planning or for efficient use of existing automation. If a change in vendor or service options is suggested by a well-conducted study, the change may be more easily accepted by the vendor and the library administration and staff.

5. *Improve Library/Vendor/Publisher Communication and Relations.* Better, more informed communication with the vendor helps identify which

problems are caused by publishers, vendors, library practices, or poor communication. Such understanding encourages serials managers to communicate appropriate complaints directly and more effectively to their sources. Publishers may welcome the opportunity to inform librarians of library or vendor practices that create difficulties for them, such as late subscription renewal authorization, inadequate monitoring for newly available standing order volumes, delayed payments, and so forth.

III. Influencing Factors and Cautions

Serials, inherently unstable and prone to multiple changes (of title, price, frequency, publisher, and address, to mention a few), present unique challenges for acquisition. These challenges are compounded by the variety of serial types, methods of supply, and the library's need to acquire each issue/volume as it is published. The multiplicity of sources, vendors, and vendor services used selectively or comprehensively by libraries adds yet another level of complexity to the acquisition process. Obviously, it is very difficult for one study to evaluate effectively total vendor performance, but understanding the complexity of the process provides perspective for the limited results of an evaluation.

The following factors should be taken into consideration when designing a methodology for evaluating serials vendors:

Measurement of Comparable Situations

Vendor evaluation criteria need to be translated into objective and measurable terms so that valid comparisons can be made. Vendor evaluations can be designed to measure changes in a single vendor's service over time, to measure one vendor's service with different types of serial orders, or to compare one vendor's performance with another's. As studies of vendors of in-print monographs have shown, the ideal situation when comparing one vendor to others is to measure identical situations: ordering the same title, at the same time, in the same place, and from all vendors to be evaluated. Because most libraries do not simultaneously order duplicate serials, attaining this ideal would be difficult. The serials "ideal" situation is to ensure that the same number of similar titles from the same publishers are considered in the performance study.

Order mix is of major significance in determining a vendor's performance and pricing on a particular account. A vendor would have no trouble servicing a list of titles from major publishers whose discounts and responsiveness would allow that vendor to offer its account prompt delivery and competitive pricing. Conversely, in trying to service a list of titles from obscure publishers that have irregular publication schedules and no available discounts, a vendor would have to assess higher charges to cover its costs of obtaining such material, if, indeed, the material was ever obtained.

Thus, if two or more vendors are to be compared, the titles selected for each sample should be matched for publisher, price, frequency of publication, and type of supply (drop-ship, which are issues mailed directly to the library from the publisher, or reship, which are issues mailed from the publisher to the vendor, then reshipped to the library). Unless each vendor handles orders from the library for the same types of publications (domestic vs. foreign, commercial publishers vs. nonprofit publishers, periodical subscriptions vs. standing orders, large vs. small presses), selecting identical samples will not be possible. Similarly, when studying a single vendor in successive years, changes in library ordering or cancellation patterns may change the order mix so that comparisons must be adjusted.

Library's Internal Procedures

A library's internal procedures and staff expertise may affect a vendor study. Variables such as the speed, accuracy, and thoroughness of recording receipts and publication information, reviewing order confirmations, and claiming missing issues can positively or negatively affect perceived vendor performance. Delivery problems may be caused by the mail delivery system. The serials manager is responsible for informing the vendor of library preferences or expectations about handling routine matters and typical problems and for communicating these requirements to library staff. Various library staff members may be unaware of conflicting instructions given to a vendor. For example, the invoice authorization clerk may prefer the original system of having credit memos issued immediately for each title, while the unit supervisor may have suggested quarterly batching of accumulated credits for ease of tracking and application. Unless feedback is provided, the vendor has no opportunity to make desired changes or explain why a practice has been changed.

Library use of a vendor-developed automated serials control system, order database, or electronic mail system can also affect staff perception of vendor performance. If the vendor-supplied system works well, the staff may generalize and perceive that vendor service is also good. The opposite may occur: problems with the system may negatively bias staff perception of overall vendor service.

Serials Types and Acquisitions

Perhaps the greatest confusion is caused by an inadequate appreciation on the part of many library staff members of the fundamental differences between periodicals and nonperiodical serials, such as annuals and irregular series. Just as the different types of serials require different acquisition techniques, their unique characteristics should also be considered in vendor performance evaluations. Techniques to study the supply of periodicals and of nonperiodical serials are provided in this guide. The supply of annual serials and other titles with regular publication frequencies can be studied much like periodicals, while irregular and monographic series supply should be studied separately, adapting techniques from periodical and monographic vendor performance evaluations.

Generally, *periodicals* are ordered in advance of publication and paid and billed as a subscription for a given volume or period, typically a year. Normally, periodicals are published on a regular schedule. Domestic periodicals are usually mailed to the library from the publisher, or drop-shipped. Foreign periodicals are also mailed as each issue is produced, but foreign vendors may choose to have the issues mailed to them for reshipment to the library. Periodical publishers expect to be paid in advance and may not renew a subscription unless payment accompanies renewal instructions.

A recent trend to print only minimal numbers in excess of paid subscriptions means that sometimes back issues are difficult to obtain, and some publishers routinely extend subscription periods in lieu of supplying claimed issues. Some publishers are unable or unwilling to enter new orders for a specific starting date; they simply begin the order with the next available issue. The subscription agent can attempt to hold orders for placement until the requested beginning date is available. Publishers rarely raise prices during the subscription period; added charges for subscriptions usually result from agents billing libraries before final price information is received from publishers or entered into vendor records, or, less frequently, from the publication of additional, unanticipated issues or volumes.

Special supply problems are associated with many types of periodicals: government documents, popular magazines, loose-leaf services, newspapers, and small press titles. Fulfillment houses handle circulation for publishers of many popular magazines. Back issues are rarely available, subscriptions are entered for the next issue (regardless of requested start date), and renewals that omit the fulfillment house coded subscription number are entered as new subscriptions. This last practice often results in gaps (skipped issues) or overlaps (duplicate issues) in supply, rather than the continuous supply that characterizes a correctly recorded renewal. Ordering such titles directly from the fulfillment house can be effective.[1]

Loose-leaf services received like periodicals may be automatically renewed. Newspapers may use midsubscription price increases to shorten the subscription term without notification; renewal notices are sent a month or less in advance of expiration and payment must be received before issues will be mailed. Purchased government serials have special ordering and billing protocols that encourage the use of deposit accounts for direct orders. Because of these special requirements, some vendors have a higher service charge for U.S. government serials. Small press titles tend to be erratic in their publication patterns.

Some *nonperiodical serials,* such as annuals, directories, and supplemental updates, behave more like periodicals than like monographs. Annuals and directories may have predictable publication patterns, most are numbered and/or dated, and most may be ordered by subscription, although billing with shipment rather than in advance is typical. Both subscription agents and standing order vendors will accept orders for these materials.

Other nonperiodical serials are irregular; the library has no notification to expect an issue or invoice. Like monographs, each volume in a monographic series has its own author and title, and the price per volume varies. The number of volumes published per year in a monographic or irregular series varies as well, and the series may be numbered or unnumbered. Proceedings may follow a regular pattern or be as unpredictable as monographic series. Proceedings and series may be purchased on a standing order, meaning each volume will be billed as issued on a volume-by-volume basis. Because the price is set close to the actual date of supply, additional charges are uncommon.

The manner of supply (drop-ship or reship) is governed by the type of material and the policy of the publisher or vendor. A given title may not be supplied in the same manner by each vendor, so a library may prefer to select a vendor whose policies regarding method of supply are in accord with library preferences. Most titles may also be ordered directly from the publisher, who thus can be evaluated like a vendor. Additional charges such as postage, handling or delivery, and the additional library processing costs required should also be taken into account in deciding when to order direct.

Serials are also produced in nonprint formats such as microforms, computer tapes and files, CD-ROMs, and as accessed online or through gateways. Sometimes the nonprint format is derived from a printed publication; in other

---

1. Marcia Tuttle, "Magazine Fulfillment Centers: What They Are, How They Operate, and What We Can Do about Them," *Library Acquisitions: Practice & Theory* 9, no. 1 (1985): 41–49.

cases, it is the sole version produced. Billing practices vary with format and may include lease arrangements, for which return to the publisher of received material is required on cancellation of the subscription. Single issue/volume and back file orders should be considered separately in evaluation studies because they represent one-time rather than ongoing orders.

Publication Schedules/Delivery

Because serials, and particularly periodicals, are usually ordered before rather than after they are published, announced issue dates and frequencies cannot be considered absolute. The publication schedules of some titles are unpredictable and irregular, and it is not uncommon for periodicals to be published late or in combined issues, while nonperiodical serials may be published out of numerical order. These publishing changes are beyond the vendor's control and may not be reported in advance by the publisher.

Subscriptions and standing orders require accurate setup for billing and shipping and an arrangement for ongoing supply/renewal. Data entry is labor-intensive and involves a high margin of error. Unlike one-time orders, speed of fulfillment may not be desired for new ongoing orders. Serial orders are often placed in advance of publication and expected to start with the first issue of a new volume or year (for periodicals) or with a specified number or imprint date (for continuations and monographic series). The library does not want to receive and pay for material that predates the specified start date, thus requiring the vendor to time orders to publishers carefully and to acknowledge order placement to the library.

In addition to publication schedules, mode of delivery is another factor to consider, especially for foreign publications. Many libraries opt for surface mail to save money but are not really prepared for the lengthy delivery time that may result. Some vendors offer special rates or types of delivery (consolidated air freight, for example) depending upon the level of business generated by the library or for an additional charge. Most large foreign publishers now use consolidated air freight for delivery of their journals to the North American continent.

The Serials Life Cycle

The ongoing nature of serials presents perhaps the greatest challenge to evaluation. An ideal study of vendor performance covers service on each portion of the life cycle of a serial:

> Is the initial order confirmed? Does it start with the correct issue, volume, or date? If not, is notification provided so a separate order can be considered while issues are still in print?

How many claims for established orders are required, and what is the
success rate?

Do subscription agent records reflect publication delays, or are renewal
payments generated without regard to publication status?

Is the subscription or standing order renewed without incurring gaps or
overlaps?

How successfully does the standing order vendor monitor publishers for
the appearance of new volumes? Are status reports issued so that
library inquiries are unnecessary? How much information is provided on the current status of standing order titles?

Are changes of title, publisher, frequency, etc., communicated in a timely
manner? Are title changes cross-referenced on reports, renewals, and
invoices?

Are significant price increases communicated to the library with sufficient lead time to effect a cancellation (if necessary) and obtain full
or prorated refunds?

Are cancellations communicated to publishers in time to avoid supply
of unwanted material? Are accurate cancellation confirmations supplied?

How are cessations and suspensions handled? How successful is the
vendor in obtaining credit for unpublished material?

IV. Qualitative Assessment and Quantitative Measures

In designing a review of vendor performance, keep in mind that both quantitative data and qualitative assessments should be considered. In the past, vendor performance evaluation consisted primarily of serials managers forming
subjective opinions about performance. Many of these opinions may have
been valid, but published studies of evaluations of monographic vendors contain some quantitative results that the authors describe as unexpected or counter-
intuitive. The few published studies of serials vendor performance are extremely
valuable, but they typically include only quantitative data.

Certain criteria that cannot be objectively and quantitatively measured,
such as the library staff's perception of the attitude and skill of the vendor's
staff, can be subjectively ranked. Such subjective rankings could have imme-
diate use at one institution but are less valid when making comparisons over
time or across institutions.

V. The Vendor Profile

Services Provided or Available

Vendors offer a wide array of services; some are included in a basic plan or package, while others may be selected with or without an additional charge. Vendor-performance studies should ensure that similar vendor services are compared:

Titles handled: Which publishers? Countries? Languages? Formats?

If a foreign vendor, can payment be made in U.S. currency? Is correspondence in English? Is there a U.S. office that can answer routine questions and forward mail and other communications?

If foreign titles are handled, how are exchange rates established? Are special shipping and/or packaging arrangements available?

Can the subscription agent handle orders for replacement issues? Back files? Can the standing order vendor handle back orders? Out-of-print searches?

What communication methods are provided? Electronic mail? Toll-free telephone number? Telefacsimile? Will collect calls be accepted?

How courteous, knowledgeable, and effective are the personnel? The sales representative? Customer service staff? Do they work effectively with library staff? Is a single customer service representative assigned to your account? If that individual is not available, is there a backup who is adequately informed? Are calls returned and correspondence answered promptly? Who initiates problem solving? Must the library make specific requests for action, such as providing proof of payment?

What is the educational level of vendor personnel? How much experience do personnel have in librarianship or library practices?

Does the vendor provide ordering guidelines? Is a catalog of publications available or a list of publishers and discount rates? Is the bibliographic information sufficient? Accurate?

What management reports are available? Can they be customized or provided in electronic format? Is there a fee?

Can invoices be provided on tape or by electronic transmission for automated systems? Is there a fee?

Are there any online services? Ordering? Claiming? What hardware or software is required or provided? Is there a fee for the service? Who pays telecommunications costs?

Service Charge and Discount Rate Assessment

Traditionally, the serials vendor has had two primary sources of income: publisher discounts and library service charges. Publishers are reducing the size of discounts for both subscriptions and standing orders to vendors and some are eliminating the practice altogether. Each library account's service charge or discount rate is typically based on its order mix and represents the amount required to supplement the income provided by publisher discounts on a library's list of titles. This is usually calculated as a percentage of the account but can be assessed in a variety of ways. The vendor's basic service charge or discount rate covers many standard services. Additional services may or may not incur additional fees.

Subscription agents typically assess a service charge, although an order mix of titles with high and low or zero discounts could be assessed a service charge of zero. Some periodical publishers who provide discounts require that their discounted titles be indicated on library subscription invoices with a zero service charge; several subscription agents have surpassed this demand and indicate service charges for each title on an invoice. Although the vendor negotiates with the library an overall service charge, knowing each title's charges is useful in monitoring publishers' discount practices.

Book vendors functioning as standing order vendors may provide either discount rates or service charges. Flat discount rates, where the same discount is applied for all titles on order, may be used. Some vendors offer and list on invoices a title-by-title (publisher-by-publisher) discount.

"Unbundling," or the "selling of vendor services individually so that libraries can choose, and pay for, the services they actually use," is not in widespread use, but vendor performance studies can be valuable in determining whether a library could benefit by unbundling.[2] For example, if a library elects to claim directly from publishers rather than through a subscription agent, the vendor's expense may be reduced and the serials manager can then negotiate for a reduction in the service charge. Although unbundling is a possible measure in lowering service charges or raising discounts, some vendors do not consider separating already integrated services an effective measure for reducing costs; rather, they suggest that prices are reduced as a result of competition rather than eliminating services.

---

2. Joseph W. Barker, "Unbundling Serials Vendors' Service Charges: Are We Ready?" *Serials Review* 16, no. 2 (1990): 34.

VI. Criteria and Techniques for Evaluation of Subscription Agents and Standing Order Vendors

Many aspects of subscription agent performance can be evaluated, although most published studies focus on only one. The evaluation of standing order vendors (used in this document for either subscription agents or book vendors regarding their supply of nonperiodical standing orders) is even less developed than that for subscription agents, with only one published study. The following categories describe key serials vendor roles and list questions to use in their evaluation. Differences between subscription agents and standing order vendors are discussed, and suggested evaluation techniques are provided in each category.

The practical studies described in this section can, in many instances, be incorporated into regular library routines to provide ongoing analysis of vendor performance. They can be conducted by libraries with manual or automated systems. One or more of these studies can be combined with a formal study to allow consideration of additional criteria.

Order Placement

Order placement refers to the initial entry of an order on behalf of the library. Orders can be for new publications, for established publications that are new to the library, or for titles that were formerly available free of charge. Libraries may also transfer titles from one vendor to another or place orders formerly ordered directly from the publisher with a vendor. Some concerns are common to both types of orders:

> Does the agent verify the accuracy and completeness of the library's order information (title, publisher and standard identification numbers, volume or publication start date, and price) and request clarification if needed?

> Are orders placed promptly? Is accurate information sent to the publisher? Are orders prepaid when required by the publisher?

> If the order is not expected to begin immediately, does the agent provide an order confirmation?

Subscription Order Placement

> Does the agent attempt to achieve the requested subscription start date by delaying order submission? By entering a separate order for back issues or volumes? Does the agent notify the library when the publisher will not honor the start date?

Are correct mailing and billing addresses and special instructions honored? If addresses must be altered to meet postal regulations or publisher fulfillment system configurations, are these changes communicated to the library?

Is the agent successful in placing multiple copy subscriptions so that the correct number of subscriptions is received, rather than additional years of a single subscription?

Standing Order Placement

There are some significant differences for standing order vendors. The requested starting date or volume can be problematical, because many titles are published out of numerical order. Asking to begin an order with a specified imprint date (i.e., year) may require the vendor to obtain additional information. Volumes may be published in a different year than was originally announced or not published at all. Reprints or revised editions may be considered "new publications" by the publisher but perhaps not by the library. Many publishers do not accept ongoing orders, so the vendor must send queries or even blind orders to determine whether any new volumes are available. Publishers require prepayment less frequently.

EVALUATION TECHNIQUES FOR BOTH TYPES OF ORDERS

Maintain an "on order file" and review it on a regular basis. Maintain statistics of numbers of total orders placed, identified by publisher, types of problems that occur, and amount of work (i.e., numbers of claims, letters, and phone calls) required by library staff to resolve those problems.

Order Renewal

Except when a major transfer of titles from one vendor to another occurs, entering new orders applies to only a fraction of titles, while order renewal should occur for all except ceased and canceled titles.

Subscription Renewal

For periodical subscriptions, the agent is expected to submit renewal orders and payments to publishers in a clear and usable format on the timetable established by each publisher. If the agent submits orders and payments separately or makes other deviations from established practice, smooth renewal may be jeopardized and a lapse in receipt can occur.

Monitoring subscription agent payments to publishers is time-consuming. Publishers' renewal notices (for subscriptions) and advertisements or solicitations (for nonperiodical serials) can be checked against library payment records, but because vendors, especially subscription agents, may bill libraries before they pay publishers, such information may indicate only the agent's intention to renew/order rather than the actual renewal. Publishers may continue to send renewal notices after receipt of subscription payment if there is any variation in customer address, if the unique subscription code is not supplied with payment, or because of internal delays in recording payments and updating files. In other cases, publisher generation of renewal notices seems totally divorced from their payment records.

1. Maintain statistics on the number of renewal notices received. This number can be monitored from year to year to indicate possible changes in prepayment patterns that may warrant more investigation.
2. If nonsupply occurs, if a delay is suspected, or if a publisher informs you that the vendor has not renewed the subscription, verify that material has been published but not received. Either examine the receipt records for other libraries (by viewing online check-in records) or contact other libraries or the publisher to determine publication schedules. (These methods can also be employed to determine the timeliness of receipt.) For lapses and delays, additional research may be required to identify the cause of untimely receipt: late publication, mail or delivery problems, or agent breakdown in service. Such investigation may be time-consuming but usually results in superior problem resolution.
3. Select a sample of publisher renewal notices. (Renewal notices received after the expected start date of the new subscription period are good candidates.) Investigate them fully and compare results from year to year.
4. Select a sample of publishers and call them to inquire about vendor renewal and prepayment practices.

Standing Order Renewal

Because publication patterns are often irregular and many publishers do not record ongoing orders, the standing order vendor is required to monitor publishers' catalogs and advertisements and/or to contact publishers on a regular basis to determine when new titles in series are available. This schedule may be several times a year, annually, or less frequently depending on the publisher, title, and vendor practice. Even when publishers do record continuing orders, the order typically indicates only the total number of copies and the vendor, not the individual library customers. Vendors may provide online or microformat access to their order files, which allows library staff to monitor activity on specific orders.

Allowing time for supply, routinely check publishers' announcements to library receipts, vendor records, or the receipt records of other libraries. Maintain statistics on the frequency with which announcements must be forwarded to the vendor.

Claims for Subscription Issues

Subscription Agents

First claims, which are the first notification libraries send to publishers and vendors of nonreceived issues, must be generated by the library for titles drop-shipped from a publisher. The agent never sees the item and must rely upon the library for notification of nonreceipt. Many agents maintain automated claiming services that regularly provide a list of claims previously requested by the library. The library staff is responsible for reviewing the list and requesting subsequent action. How an agent processes claims also affects how successfully the claimed issues are received:

> Are claims from libraries simply forwarded to publishers or reviewed and compared to publisher information about combined issues, delays, or dispatch data?
>
> Does the agent verify the library's order for the claimed title and confirm that payment has been made to the publisher?
>
> Do claims provide publishers with all necessary information (such as the enumeration and chronology of the material, complete subscriber address and payment information, correct title and order codes, or other information required by the publisher)?
>
> How soon after receipt from the library does the agent review and submit claims to publishers?
>
> Are claims acknowledged (individually; on a consolidated report)?

1. Ask the agent's staff to explain how claims are processed, using the questions in this section.
2. Maintain copies or lists of library-generated first claims; check them against agent- or library-generated lists to monitor agent accuracy and subsequent action.
3. Check successive versions of an agent's list against prior versions to see that all active claims are listed and requested action was taken.

4. Determine the time lag between library submission of a claim and the agent's transmittal to the publisher. See if the agent's records (either claim reports or online databases) include the date on which the staff forwarded a claim to the publisher. If so, then copy a sample of library-generated claims with the dates of dispatch to the agent. Subsequently, check the agent's report for each claim in the sample and note the date it was forwarded to the publisher. If the library's practice is to send claims by first class mail, also send a sample of claims by telefacsimile or electronic mail. Repeat this process every three or four months for a year. Data analysis should indicate (a) the average time it took for the agent to review and forward claims to the publisher and whether or not this matches the agent's assessment of the time required and (b) how long it takes for the claims to reach the agent using first class mail and whether another transmission method is preferable.

5. Annotate each title on a list for first, second, and repeated claims. Maintain an entire year's worth for later analysis. If agents do not supply lists or if multiple agents are being studied, then maintain statistics that identify for each agent first claims, second claims, and third and later claims. Record response rates for information and material received for each of the three categories of claims. Analyze the results annually. The results may indicate that purchasing replacements earlier instead of continuing to reclaim is more successful in obtaining missing issues and more cost-effective in terms of staff time.

6. The data collected can be analyzed to produce two measures of effectiveness. The *claim response rate* refers to the number of claims for which a response was received (even a response like "claimed after deadline, must purchase separately"). The *claim success rate* is a subset of the response rate; this is the number of claims successfully resolved, that is, for which claimed material was received. In parallel to the fulfillment rate, both the response and success rate can be calculated by the number of issues received compared to the number of issues published.

Standing Order Vendors

Most claims for standing order material can be considered under the renewal category in which new material is not truly on order and must be solicited. The claims category is better utilized for materials that have been ordered, according to vendor reports, or even invoiced but have not been received by the library.

EVALUATION TECHNIQUE

Maintain statistics on the incidence when material is reported as available, on order, or invoiced but must be claimed before receipt.

Order Fulfillment

Fulfillment is of critical importance, but unless the publisher provides an explanation (such as "issue/volume never published"), extensive research may be required to determine where the problem occurred and what caused it. Because periodicals are usually shipped by the publisher, rather than the vendor, it may be difficult to evaluate the vendor's role in fulfillment. Possibilities include delivery system failure, change in publisher, late library renewal authorization, inaccurate library order information, inaccurate vendor payment, and incorrect application of payment by publisher, or some combination of these and similar problems. No one entity in the fulfillment chain has complete information, and sometimes no conclusive explanation can be identified. Although the cause of nonreceipt cannot always be determined, the fact of nonreceipt is somewhat easier to assess. Fulfillment can be measured by calculating the ratio of material received to material published.

Subscription Fulfillment

Comparing the number of items received to the number of items published on subscription is less simple than it sounds. The problem occurs in identifying exactly what was published and when; if material was not received, one generally cannot determine from local files how many items were published. (For example, a "monthly" may constitute six double issues, or eight monthly issues and two double issues, or other variations.) The ambiguous nature of fulfillment should be considered when analyzing data.

Standing Order Fulfillment

Although the order and supply mechanisms are different, standing order fulfillment can be evaluated by similar means.

EVALUATION TECHNIQUE FOR BOTH TYPES OF ORDERS

Record all instances when material is not obtained and indicate the cause of the problem, when identified. Keep separate statistics for material that was successfully reordered (distinguished from a claim by the need for a second payment) and for material that was unavailable (out-of-print) despite reordering, including the cost per item. Include publisher names in these records. If a total number of items received from the vendor is available, compare the two totals to calculate the fulfillment percentage. Analyze the reasons for nonsupply annually and provide a copy of the report to the vendor.

Condition of Material on Receipt

Drop-Shipped Subscription Issues

Subscription agents can convey claims for the replacement of damaged material and request changes in publisher practice to avoid problems in the future. Receipt problems (such as poor label attachment, light cover stock titles mailed without a protective cover or enclosure, or inadequate binding) should be reported to the agent. The agent can then request improvements from publishers; the library may also choose to complain directly to publishers.

EVALUATION TECHNIQUE

Maintain statistics on the total number of replacement requests made for damaged material. Determine the success rate. Monitor whether offending publishers change their practices.

Reshipped Issues and Volumes

For reshipped titles only, vendors are responsible for the physical condition of the shipments (adequate packing and wrapping), accuracy of address, completeness and correctness of shipment (conformity with packing slip and no duplication), and fulfillment of special requirements (invoice included with shipment or sent separately).

EVALUATION TECHNIQUE

Maintain statistics on the total number of shipments received, with categories to record the frequency of each type of problem.

Fair and Accurate Pricing

Price is one of the most significant criteria to evaluate. An advantageous service charge or a seemingly generous "flat discount" applied to inflated prices is no bargain, so the library must first determine that pricing is fair and accurate. Vendor incentives to libraries and publisher incentives to vendors for early payment can also affect the price paid by the library. For many titles, a publisher list price is established and that price is charged for each item (subscription, volume, etc.) ordered through a vendor. For other titles, how the publisher or vendor handles publisher discounts or foreign exchange rates can affect the price charged. Publishers or vendors also make errors in billing, particularly when multiple rates (membership, package discount, institutional or geographic location differentiation) are available.

A related aspect is the way prices are determined in bid situations. A vendor can supply its pricing formula, but without the actual list price of the next volume, the price a vendor provides on a bid is only an estimate. When the list price is unknown, vendors often use the list price of the previously supplied volume as a basis for prices quoted on bids. This practice may penalize vendors who update price information more quickly. Some vendors may also selectively eliminate unprofitable items from a library's list in hopes of being awarded only the profitable titles.

> Are serials' prices charged in accord with prices listed in the issues or volumes or publishers' announcements and catalogs?

> What is the vendor's policy on publisher discounts? In which situations can discounts reduce charges for specific titles (e.g., continuations, popular magazines, zero discount titles, specific publishers)? Does the subscription agent pay publishers early enough to obtain maximum discounts? Does the agent pass on publisher early payment discount offers?

> How are foreign exchange rates calculated? When the publisher doesn't set the rate, how does the agent determine it? What date is used to determine the exchange rate: when billed by the publisher, by the agent, the date of payment by the library, or date of receipt of payment? (Major vendors recommend that a three-to-five year period be considered in evaluating policies and performance on exchange rates.)

> Does the agent offer early payment discounts? Is the interest rate competitive and/or negotiable? Can the agent accept bank-to-bank transfers to facilitate meeting an early payment deadline?

> Can the interest earned be credited in a variety of ways (e.g., credit memo, adjustment of service charge, or application to special services)? For foreign vendors, can the library request that its prepayment be credited in U.S. dollars or another currency?

> Does the agent advise of combination rates when ordering titles available in combination?

1. Pricing options and policies can be determined by asking vendors to respond to a written request for information, using questions from the list in this section.
2. Verifying prices for titles is also recommended; particularly for titles with multiple rates (foreign, membership, packages, etc.), the invoiced price should be compared to the price listed in the publisher's catalog or that given in the item itself. A sample of titles can be checked; if discrepancies are identified, review of additional titles and confirmation with publishers may be warranted. Currency conversion based on the *Wall Street Journal* exchange rate for the month of invoicing may be used for smaller publishers, while large publishers typically publicize

the rate they employ. This review should be conducted annually. For subscription agents, wait until all added charges are billed and posted. Inflating list prices is a serious charge; your vendor should be given the opportunity to respond to evidence you collect.

Verification of Service Charge, Discount Rate

Service charges and publisher discounts are the two primary sources of serials vendor income. The service charge is usually expressed as a percentage of the value of the total library account but may be calculated in many ways. When a vendor sets a discount rate for standing orders, it may be either a flat rate for the entire account or vary by publisher to reflect their discounts to the vendor. Discounts for standing orders are usually determined by the number of standing orders, often taking into account the volume of firm orders and approval sales as well as publisher discounts. Ideally, the service charge or discount rate should reflect the cost to the vendor of handling orders for the library and allow a reasonable profit. Librarians and vendors believe that service charge fees are lower than the anticipated library costs in staff time for performing these services in-house. Most vendors are willing to negotiate charges, while some have a set rate. In an increasingly competitive marketplace, it is good business practice to understand how service charges and discount rates are calculated and to verify them.

Subscription and Standing Order
Service Charges and Discount Rates

> What is the actual composite service charge or discount rate when added charges or adjusted billings, supplemental billings, continuations, reinstatements, and other transactions are incorporated?

> Do credits include the same service charge or discount rate? Always? Or only when the agent made an error?

> Will the vendor consider unbundling service charges or discount rates and allow you to negotiate for a better rate if not all services are used?

Subscription Services Charges Only

> How is the service charge determined? Is anything other than order mix considered? Is unbundling an option? How are "zero service charge" journal subscriptions handled? (Several major commercial scientific/technical/medical publishers have informed agents that because they provide substantial discounts to the agents, their titles should

not be assessed service charges.) Are these titles included in the library's overall account mix? Is the service charge for each title on an invoice itemized? What is the actual charge for the nonzero service charge titles?

Is there a cap on service charges for expensive titles (e.g., the maximum is 4 percent or $50, whichever is lower)? Is there a minimum charge per title (e.g., for a $20 title, the minimum charge is $5, or 25 percent; or it is not set and may be $20, or 100 percent)?

Is there a "per line charge"? Are multiple year or multiple copy orders entered as separate invoice lines, each incurring a service charge, or are they combined into a single invoice line with a single service charge?

Standing Order Discount Rates Only

How is the discount computed? Is it based solely on title mix and quantity of standing orders, or are firm orders and approval sales also considered?

Are postage and handling included or excluded?

Is the discount negotiable based on service provided?

EVALUATION TECHNIQUES

1. Ask the vendor to explain the service charge or discount rate policy, using questions in this section.
2. Examine invoices for actual charges and discounts and calculate an overall rate for the entire account over a full year. If you find discrepancies, obtain an explanation and/or an adjustment.

Invoice and Credit Activity

Invoices should contain accurate and complete library and title information, clearly presented in a format that can be used by the library. Library-specific information typically includes the following items for subscriptions, which may be adjusted for local needs: vendor payment address, library address (with separate shipping and billing addresses), account number(s), order numbers, tax charges, fund names or codes, and call numbers. Title listings should include information adequate to identify the title and material being billed: title, previous title (if a change has occurred within the last 12 months), ISSN, accurate price, and enumeration and/or date coverage of the billing. Vendor title numbers are usually included as well. The flexibility and sophistication of invoicing arrangements should also be considered.

Subscription and Standing Order Invoices

What efficiencies does the vendor achieve by electronic data interchange with publishers (e.g., exchanging renewal and pricing information by electronic or machine-readable tapes or providing library invoices in machine-readable form)?

Are credits supplied promptly, or is library follow-up required? Is a credit schedule (individual, quarterly, etc.) available? Do credit memos contain the same types of accurate and complete information as invoices?

Are statements timely, accurate, and clearly presented? Do they reflect current account status or are problems previously explained listed repeatedly?

Can service charges or discount rates, postage, and handling be itemized for each title or summarized for the entire invoice? Can such charges be incorporated into each title's charge?

How are foreign currency prices represented? Can the original foreign price and the U.S. dollar price be shown? Is the exchange rate listed on the invoice?

Subscription Invoices Only

Are flexible billing arrangements for subscriptions available? Can early renewal be requested for expensive subscriptions to reserve rates before increases take effect?

What methods can the agent offer to minimize added charges and supplemental invoices? Can the agent bill only after final publisher rates or invoices are received? Can such final charges be batched for monthly or quarterly billing? Is it possible to receive an "estimated" invoice early in the renewal cycle that can be paid but not posted to individual titles, with a "final" invoice supplied after firm prices are received from publishers? How accurate is the estimate? What percentage of titles require added charge billing?

Complete information about special rates or subscription packages should be included (e.g., all titles included on membership subscriptions, special discounts, and related information).

Standing Order Invoices Only

Information about the shipment should include for each volume the series title and ISSN, number in the series, title of the individual volume (when appropriate), its ISBN, number of a multipart work, information about the reprint status or particular edition, and price. Discount rates or service charges and special terms such as return deadlines and nonreturnable status should be included.

Depending on the agreement between the library and the vendor, the invoice should be included with the shipment or supplied separately.

EVALUATION TECHNIQUE

Develop a reporting system for use during the payment process as problems are encountered. Missing information need not be reported unless a problem is caused by its absence. Examine a year's worth of reports and a sample of invoices and credits. Identify practices that cause problems. Discuss concerns with the vendor.

Database Quality and Automated Services

The accuracy and promptness with which the vendor database is maintained affects all of the categories discussed in this section. Similarly, the vendor's use of automation and ability to interact with library automated systems represent important services.

Does the vendor supply status reports that eliminate the need for some claims and research about possible title changes, new subscription packages, and other changes in the material received? Are these reports timely? Can the vendor customize reports to list only your titles?

Is electronic access to the vendor's database available? How user friendly is access? Is there a fee?

What support for library automation is available? Are appropriate standards, such as the MAchine Readable Cataloging (MARC) format for bibliographic information and American National Standards Institute (ANSI) standards for telecommunications, supported? Is the vendor committed to supporting new standards as they are developed? Can the vendor accept orders and claims electronically? Does the vendor's system interface with the library's integrated library system? Can the vendor supply invoices on tape or electronically?

If management reports are available, is the information helpful and presented in a usable format? Can management reports be provided in machine-readable form? Are customized reports available? What is the charge, if any, for management reports?

Question the vendor, using these questions. Maintain notes on instances when performance does not meet expectations and share this information with the vendor.

Annual Account Review

Libraries that routinely check annual account renewal lists against receipt and payment records to make renewal authorization decisions for each title can, with minor adjustments, create an annual snapshot of many types of account activity. The same type of review can be conducted using the main annual renewal invoice or a list of titles on order with a specific vendor maintained by the library. This review is dependent on the amount of information maintained in library records.

EVALUATION TECHNIQUE

The library serials manager establishes a list of codes and writes instructions for staff describing which types of activities are to be identified and recorded in code. For example, code categories may include whether a title has current outstanding claims, old outstanding claims, or claims successfully resolved during the year (assuming records for successful claims are maintained). Codes can be created for any recorded type of activity.

The list is then compared, title by title, to receipt and payment records. As claims or problems are detected, the reviewer writes the appropriate code or codes on the renewal. When the list is completely checked, the percentages of types of claims, billing problems, or other problems can be calculated. The process is easier in subsequent years, when staff can first compare the new list to the previous year's completed list to identify differences in entry, determine whether requested cancellations and new orders have been processed, and ensure that title changes are not listed twice (under old and new forms). The total number of problems and their percentages of total orders can be compared with those of previous renewals.

Interaction with Library

This category considers the training, resources, skill, and courtesy of the vendor's staff (account representative, sales representative, and other personnel); quality of communication with the library; volume and type of correspondence required; overall problem resolution rate; and the length of time required for resolution. Although the techniques are more subjective, this information can be discussed during sales representative visits and used as supplemental documentation for a formal vendor performance evaluation.

Evaluation Techniques

1. Ask staff to participate in preparing a checklist for vendor evaluation (sample questions follow). Distribute printed copies and ask each person to rank the performance on a scale of one to five. Discuss the perceptions as a group and determine consensus rankings. Repeat this process several times a year, perhaps to coincide with vendor visits.

   > How good is the attitude, cooperation, and knowledge of the vendor's staff? Is a single account representative assigned and available? Is a backup available and knowledgeable?

   > Are phone calls returned promptly and written queries attended to without additional follow-up? Do promised actions occur in a timely manner? Do customer service staff monitor their own performance by frequent contact with the library?

   > Does the sales representative take the initiative to consult the library to discuss service problems and information about new services? Does she or he visit the library as needed?

   > How effective are the communication devices provided or made available (e.g., toll-free phone number, toll-free facsimile number, electronic mail)?

   > Can the vendor establish and follow a service profile so standing instructions need not be reiterated (e.g., extra charge supplements, additional volumes, indexes, etc., must be advised and terms accepted rather than automatically supplied; orders cannot be billed more than three years in advance of current receipt; orders with no billing for three years are considered canceled and must be reinstated)?

   > Are reasonable adjustments made for disputed charges and nonsupply?

   > Does the vendor attempt to honor occasional special requests (e.g., attempts to obtain credit for a "no cancellation" or "no return" title)?

2. Problems that require original correspondence (rather than a telephone call, form letter, or electronic mail) are a good indication of vendor performance. Maintain a file of this correspondence, add information about outcomes, and evaluate it regularly for frequency of types of problems and resolution rate.

27

Interaction with Publisher

A vendor's interaction with a publisher is essential to any transaction performed and underlies many of the evaluation categories. The library should be aware of the margin of error in each category of performance under review and establish methods for viewing vendor/publication details on request. For example, information such as the date of the initial order, renewal authorization, and payments sent to the publisher, with verification of receipt by the publisher (such as a list of checks and the dates they were cashed), function as an "audit trail" for the evaluation process. Admittedly neither library nor vendor would want to communicate all these details routinely for every title ordered, but access to such information allows the evaluation of where collapses are in the "service communication chain."

EVALUATION TECHNIQUE

If problems occur, ask the vendor to supply information to determine the interaction with the publisher in the situation. Call the publisher if you need additional information. If you determine that the vendor is at fault, discuss this with the vendor and ask for a change in practice if that seems warranted.

VII. Methodologies: Formal Studies

Although most published formal studies focus on a few criteria, it is theoretically possible to design and conduct comprehensive studies that evaluate the complete range of vendor activity. Such studies are likely to be complicated and time-consuming unless appropriate automation support is available. A serials manager will most likely decide to conduct a formal study of selected criteria based on local needs and available support. This section describes such a process. Designing a formal study requires three stages: planning and preparation, execution, and analysis.

Planning and Preparation

Overview

In the first stage, identify why a study is needed and what it is expected to reveal. Analyze the local situation to determine what staffing and data-collection resources are available. Consider the scope of the study in terms of the time period examined and number of titles studied. Consult an expert on research methodologies, such as a statistician or expert in data analysis.

To identify the reasons for the study and anticipated application, answering questions like these will be helpful:

Is a study necessary?

What are the reasons for conducting a study?

Does the library expect to place subscriptions on bid so that having data comparing vendor services is needed?

Would it be useful to establish a baseline for current performance before work flow changes are made?

What data can be collected to measure improvement?

Does the current service charge seem high for the services received or as it compares to other vendors' charges?

Does the current claim response rate seem unsatisfactory?

To analyze local circumstances regarding staffing and data collection, answering these questions will be helpful:

What data are already collected or readily available?

What data can be collected with some additional work or by revising procedures?

What data can only be collected with significant involvement of staff time?

Who will collect the data?

If data will not be collected as a by-product of another procedure, what level of staff and amount of time will be needed for collection?

Can existing staff handle data collection duties, or are other arrangements needed?

Consider the scope of the study in terms of duration and titles studied:

Is it to be a one-time study or an ongoing or reproducible procedure?

How long will the study last?

Should the entire vendor list or a sample be studied?

The smallest statistically valid sample is 100; how will samples be selected?

What kind of data analysis is anticipated?

It is strongly recommended that the serials manager discuss the project with an expert in statistics and data analysis during the planning process. Good sources may be found among computer center staff, college or university faculty, or library colleagues. Advice, for instance, on sample selection and on designing a data collection form that can be coded for computerized data entry can save time and ensure a valid study. If statistical analysis is to be done, experts can suggest which test would be the most appropriate and determine if data collection will support that method of analysis. They may also suggest that no elaborate analysis is appropriate.

Execution

In the second stage, sampling is completed, instructions are prepared, and data are collected and collated. The serials manager must exercise appropriate supervision and review of the entire project to ensure valid results.

Sample selection is carefully devised in the "planning and preparation" segment. Because the validity of the results is based on the validity of the sample, accurate sampling is crucial to the success of a study. The serials manager should monitor the sampling process to determine that valid assumptions have been made and that instructions are followed. (For example, if a random sample is to be selected by choosing the twentieth title on each page of an invoice and some pages are found to contain fewer than twenty titles, the methodology is flawed and must be revised.) Another action that can affect sample validity is changing the number or types of orders assigned to particular vendors during the course of the study. Such changes may be caused by vendors (a vendor going out of business or being purchased by another firm, for example) or by the library (through cancellations or by transferring titles from one vendor to another). These types of transfers will generate more "start-up" problems than the renewal of orders through the same vendor.

Consistency in data collection is of paramount importance. Instructions must be clear to all staff, and a pretest is recommended. Any changes needed should be incorporated into the written instructions. Once the study is under way, one person should be responsible for making and communicating decisions about exceptions and additional criteria.

If the study continues for more than a few weeks, review the methodology and preliminary results at established points in the study. Any number of unanticipated problems may occur, and it is important that they be identified and corrected at an early stage to avoid jeopardizing the validity of the conclusions.

Analysis

Assuming that expert statistical advice has been followed and the study has been accurately conducted, data analysis should be relatively straightforward. Quantitative data can be analyzed using standard statistical analysis techniques described in the *Guide to Performance Evaluation of Library Materials Vendors* (pp. 7–10).

Note should be taken of any special circumstances that may have affected the study, such as a postal strike, resignation of a key staff member, change in titles placed with the vendor, newly automated systems, systems upgrades, or changes in the institution's mailroom, accounting office, etc.

The results of the study may warrant one or more actions. If the results are inconclusive or the study is found to be defective, perhaps the best action is to incorporate changes into the study methodology and conduct a new study. The survey may identify library procedures that should be changed. Even if the study results are dramatic and seem to indicate differences between vendors, variations in the vendor profiles should be considered before any action is taken. Vendors will appreciate the opportunity to respond to survey results.

After careful analysis of the survey results and information supplied by the vendor, additional action may be warranted: reassignment of certain types of orders, consolidation of orders with better rated vendors, and/or negotiation for changes in the service charge, for example. These actions are frequently taken without conducting a study of vendor performance. However, when such changes are supported by the results of a good vendor performance survey, they are more easily accepted by vendors, library staff, and administrators.

VIII. Disclosure of Evaluation Results

Comparisons of vendors between libraries must be approached with caution. Each library's internal processes, requirements, and preferences are unique; therefore, factors affecting one may not apply to another. A methodology must be consistently applied to achieve results, which then can fruitfully be shared with others, but even then many believe that vendors should not be named in published reports. Similar caution is advised when orally sharing the results of a vendor performance study with colleagues.

On the other hand, informed consumers can be eager to compare notes with colleagues and to share what they have learned with other serial managers who have not conducted vendor performance studies. Those choosing to share such information are advised to include cautionary remarks about the complex nature of vendor profiles and library needs that make each relationship between vendor and library unique. Serials managers receiving information about vendor performance evaluations at other institutions are similarly responsible for understanding that one should never assume that the results of another library's performance evaluation are transferable to one's own institution.

IX. Conclusion

The purpose of this guide is to promote better evaluation of serials vendors and standing order vendors and appropriate use of study results. The ALCTS Serials Section Acquisitions Committee recommends that vendor evaluation be incorporated into the regular work flow and that clear objectives for vendor performance be established and communicated to vendors.

Vendor performance evaluation studies need to be tailored to each library's environment. Particular care must be taken to ensure only comparable situations are directly compared. The vendor being studied should be provided with full results and allowed to respond. Serials managers are encouraged to share their study methodologies and results with colleagues in appropriate and responsible ways, while those receiving study results are charged to apply similar precautions.

Effective studies that include both quantitative and qualitative measurements should result in the following benefits:

1. Assurance of full vendor compliance with the terms and conditions established for doing business
2. Better service to library clientele
3. Improved accountablilty for expenditure of library funds
4. Improved vendor performance
5. Identification of the optimal combination of service provided and service charge or discount rate structure assessed
6. More timely and complete order fulfillment and improved status reports
7. Improved library procedures and better management information
8. Improved library/vendor/publisher communication and relations.

Selected Bibliography

This bibliography focuses primarily on articles that relate to selection and evaluation of serials vendors. Therefore, articles dealing strictly with monographic vendor studies have been excluded, with one or two exceptions. These exceptions contain information that is pertinent to anyone considering undertaking a project to evaluate serials vendors. The articles are grouped into two main categories: those that describe how a subscription agency functions, or should function, and those that focus on vendor selection and evaluation.

Annotations were prepared and sources compiled by members of the Serials Section Acquisitions Committee. Some sources and annotations were taken from *A Bibliography of Library Acquisitions* by James T. Deffenbaugh and Hope H. Yelich, revised, 1991, by Barbara Dean for the Resources Section, Acquisitions Committee; *Guide to Performance Evaluation of Library Materials Vendors* (Chicago: ALA, 1988); and "The Development of Criteria and Methodologies for Evaluating the Performance of Monograph and Serials Vendors" by October Ivins (*Advances in Serials Management* 2 [1988]).

How a Subscription Agency Functions

Baldwin, Jane, and Arlene Moore Sievers. "Subscription Agents and Libraries: An Inside View of What Every Serials Librarian Should Know." *Advances in Serials Management* 2 (1988): 37–45.

>Coauthored by two people who have worked for serial agents, this article discusses libraries' and agencies' relationships from the agent's perspective. An "educated consumer" serves the library best and has a better working relationship with an agency. Communication on both sides ensures a better understanding of the libraries' needs and the outside forces controlling the agency. The article suggests visiting the agent's office, asking questions, making the library's needs known, and making efforts to know one another. "The challenge to both librarians and agents is to make the relationship more open as well as more effective."

Basch, N. Bernard. "The Business of Subscription Agencies: A Look at Maximizing Profitability." *Library Acquisitions: Practice & Theory* 13, no. 2 (1989): 129–31.

> When selecting subscription agencies, librarians should make educated decisions based not on habit or tradition, but price and services that meet the library's needs. Overheads for agencies are high, but profit lies in volume: spreading "heavy investment and maintenance charges over millions of transactions." Publishers, on the other hand, view "libraries as a difficult market." Publishers' profits lie in advertising, not service to libraries, and their discounts to agencies vary from 30 percent to 0 percent. Agencies' service charges are calculated based on the mix of titles on a subscription list (some with discounts, some without). When looking for or evaluating an agency, the librarian should be "an educated consumer."

Basch, N. Bernard. "Determining Which Subscription Agency Services Best Meet Your Needs." *Serials Librarian* 17, no. 3/4 (1990): 81–85.

> Reviews the factors that play a significant role in determining which agent to use: price (service charge), hidden costs (such as unfavorable interest return on prepayment), what services the vendor can perform more cost-effectively than the library, and their cost. In summary, "it is important to determine which services are critical to the operations of the library, which vendor offers the best support for such essential functions, and to negotiate for the required services at an acceptable price."

Basch, N. Bernard, and Judy McQueen. *Buying Serials: A How-to-Do-It Manual for Librarians.* New York: Neal-Schuman, 1990.

> The emphasis on this most welcome addition to the serials literature is the serials acquisitions process, with chapters on "Subscription Agencies," "The Subscription Agency Business," "Choosing an Agency," and "Using an Agency." The authors provide excellent and practical in-depth coverage of these topics.

Cargill, Jennifer. "The Vendor Services Supermarket: The New Consumerism." *Wilson Library Bulletin* 57, no. 5 (1983): 394–400.

> Discusses two trends: the declining number of vendors and how "service has become a product in itself, varying in sophistication and complexity from company to company." The article advocates an active consumerism on the part of librarians that recognizes the importance of evaluation and offers ideas for communicating, not conducting, evaluations.

Clasquin, Frank F. "The Fiduciary Relationship of Libraries and Subscription Agencies. " *Serials Librarian* 17, no. 1/2 (1989): 39–43.

> A discussion of the contractual steps in order placement between (1) the library and the agency; (2) the agency, on the library's behalf, with the

publisher; (3) the library and the publisher; and (4) the trust assumed by all parties. Deals with the contractual agreement, often overlooked, of the publisher with fulfillment centers that handle orders for the publisher. The author stresses the need for libraries and librarians to be fully familiar with an agency's services.

Green, Paul Robert. "The Performance of Subscription Agents: A Detailed Survey." *Serials Librarian* 8, no. 2 (1983): 7–22.

This article is a follow-up to an earlier survey that evaluated agents' performance by comparing the number of claims sent over a period of time and calculating the number of claims per title. This study tracks claims per issues expected instead of claims per title. The number of claims is compared to the number of expected issues, then further divided by the number of first, second, and third claims. This analysis is intended to reveal the efficiency of agents in dealing with claims and ranks the agencies accordingly. Agent rank differs depending on which method of comparison is used. Concludes that claims per issue is a more reliable indicator of performance.

Huff, William H. "Serial Subscription Agents." *Library Trends* 24, no. 4 (1976): 683–709.

Covers history, function, costs, and marketing factors. Also analyzes the impact of the growth in the number of serials and trends in library cooperation on the subscription industry.

Ivins, October. "Do Subscription Agencies Earn Their Service Charges and How Can We Tell?" *Library Acquisitions: Practice & Theory* 13, no. 2 (1989): 143–47.

Derived from a paper presented at the 1988 Charleston Conference, this article lists eleven assumptions "based on . . . opinion and practical considerations." Discusses services provided by vendors, service charges, and how service charges are computed. Encourages librarians to become "informed consumers" and to speak up and become "squeaky wheels" when negotiating for their respective libraries.

Ivins, October. "We Need Department Store and Boutique Serials Vendors." *Serials Librarian* 17, no. 3/4 (1990): 99–106.

Elaborates on six reasons why multiple vendors should be used, advises under what circumstances vendor assignment should be reviewed, and identifies some factors libraries may want to consider in evaluating vendor performance.

Kent, Philip G. "How to Evaluate Serials Suppliers." *Library Acquisitions: Practice & Theory* 18, no. 1 (1994): 83–87.

Considers that price and service are the two criteria in evaluating serials suppliers. Discusses briefly how prices (service charges) are determined by vendors. Lists several categories to be considered for services and suggests some techniques for implementing evaluation of these.

Merriman, John B. "Subscription Agents—Are They Worth Their Salt?" *Library Acquisitions: Practice & Theory* 13, no. 2 (1989): 149–52.

Brief overview of what libraries should expect from their subscription agents, services agents provide for publishers, and factors agents consider when pricing service charges. Also cites the leading six criteria librarians look for when choosing an agent (based on a study sponsored by the Association of Research Libraries of its member libraries).

Merriman, John B. "The Work of a Periodicals Agent." *Serials Librarian* 14, no. 3/4 (1988): 17–36.

Examines the relationship between agents, libraries, and publishers. Defines what the "good" agent must do and describes how an agency handles the library's account. This article contains much valuable information that could be used in a vendor evaluation study.

Vendor Selection and Evaluation

American Library Association. *Guide to Performance Evaluation of Library Materials Vendors.* Acquisition Guidelines no. 5. Chicago: American Library Association, 1988.

Thorough checklist of questions to ask in an evaluation. Includes various approaches to statistical analysis. Also suggests how to approach this process if you have an automated system. Good bibliography included. Used as a starting point for the *Guide to Performance Evaluation of Serials Vendors.*

Association for Higher Education. Acquisitions Subcommittee of the Library Committee. The Vendor Study Group. "Vendor Evaluations: A Selected Annotated Bibliography, 1955–1987." *Library Acquisitions: Practice & Theory* 12, no. 1 (1988): 17–28.

A selective annotated bibliography covering 1955–1987 that evaluates vendors (serials, monographs, and publishers). It is divided into two parts: (1) methodologies and studies and (2) supporting materials. The bibliography does not include citations covering approval plans.

Barker, Joseph W. "Random Vendor Assignment in Vendor Performance Evaluation." *Library Acquisitions: Practice & Theory* 10, no. 4 (1986): 265–80.

Report of a comprehensive monograph vendor evaluation project at the University of California–Berkeley Library. Though the breadth of the project may be beyond the capacities of most libraries, it provides some excellent methodological insights, both for establishing and executing the goals of the evaluation. Provides helpful examples of vendor selections, coding, adaption of automated systems, and treatment of special issues. Illustrative tables and graphs supplied.

Bonk, Sharon C. "Toward a Methodology of Evaluating Serials Vendors." *Library Acquisitions: Practice & Theory* 9, no. 1 (1985): 51–60.

Provides a thorough discussion of the thought process and analysis necessary to devise a serials vendor evaluation. Identifies the components in evaluating serials vendors. The study described excludes periodicals, newspapers, and loose-leaf services and was performed in cooperation with 12 other academic/research libraries.

Derthick, Jan, and Barbara B. Moran. "Serial Agent Selection in ARL Libraries." *Advances in Serials Management* 1 (1986): 1–42.

An excellent article on serials vendor selection practice by the Association of Research Libraries. The authors conducted a survey to "investigate present-day attitudes" of libraries about subscription agency services and "the criteria upon which libraries base their vendor selection." Provides a thorough review (now dated) of the literature. Copy of questionnaire included.

Ivins, October. "The Development of Criteria for Evaluating Vendor Performance of Monograph and Serial Vendors." *Advances in Serials Management* 2 (1988): 185–212.

Examines the literature on evaluating performance of monograph and serial vendors. The limited amount of published material on serial vendor performance evaluation is noted. Particular vendor performance studies are cited, and formation of a group of standards is advocated.

Joseph, Rosamma. "Procurement of Foreign Periodicals Direct and Through Agents." *Library Progress* 3 (1983): 37–42.

A comparison by two libraries in India of the procurement of the same foreign titles (e.g., American and European)—one using an agent and the other ordering directly from the publisher. Comparative efficiency was gauged by time lag in the receipt of periodicals and the completion of volumes. The study calculated the libraries' cost per title and determined that ordering from the publisher is more efficient and economical. Library staff and procurement costs were not considered.

Kuntz, Harry. "Serials Agents: Selection and Evaluation." *Serials Librarian* 2, no. 2 (1977): 139–50.

Guidelines to use in deciding whether to use subscription agents; the
evaluation mentioned in the title is related to selection and not to performance.

McDonough, Joyce. "Planning, Conducting, and Analyzing Serials Vendor
Performance Studies." *Serials Librarian* 19, no. 3/4 (1991): 221–23.

Report of a workshop conducted by October Ivins and Mary McLaren
at North American Serials Interest Group (NASIG). Ivins reviews factors, both objective and subjective, to consider. McLaren describes a
study conducted at the University of Kentucky evaluating the transfer of
titles to a new vendor. They developed weighted criteria (which are
specified in the article and could be invaluable to others) to use in their
deliberations.

McKinley, Margaret. "Vendor Selection: Strategic Choices." *Serials Review*
16, no. 2 (1990): 49–53, 64.

Although not specifically on vendor performance evaluation, this article gives excellent advice on the placement of serial subscription orders
and how appropriate order strategies and vendor selection can reduce
later payment and receipt problems. Includes ordering strategies for
periodicals, newspapers, continuations, documents, loose-leaf services,
foreign publications, gifts, and exchanges.

Pilling, Stella. "The Use of Serial Subscription Agents by the British Library
Document Supply Centre." *Serials Librarian* 14, no. 3/4 (1988) : 127–31.

BLDSC uses 13 subscription agencies to obtain more than 70 percent of
their serials. Two reasons are given for using agents: convenience and
cost-effectiveness. The library needs to monitor its agents' performance
for several reasons and mentions several aspects of performance that
could be analyzed.

Schmidt, Karen A. "Choosing a Serials Vendor." *Serials Librarian* 14, no. 3/4
(1988): 11–15.

The article discusses five criteria to consider in choosing a serials vendor: service, automation, discounts, fees, and persona. Lack of training
and information on the part of the librarian often occurs. No methodology for evaluating is given.

Thornton, S. A., and C. J. Bigger. "Periodicals, Prices and Policies." *Aslib
Proceedings* 37, no. 11/12 (Nov./Dec. 1985): 437–52.

Results of a survey regarding subscription prices paid by 86 libraries for
titles ordered through 19 different agencies. Includes checklist of items
to consider in evaluating performance but no methodology.